Ladislav Burita

Information Systems in Education

Ladislav Burita

Information Systems in Education

LAP LAMBERT Academic Publishing

Impressum / Imprint

Bibliografische Information der Deutschen Nationalbibliothek: Die Deutsche Nationalbibliothek verzeichnet diese Publikation in der Deutschen Nationalbibliografie; detaillierte bibliografische Daten sind im Internet über http://dnb.d-nb.de abrufbar.
Alle in diesem Buch genannten Marken und Produktnamen unterliegen warenzeichen-, marken- oder patentrechtlichem Schutz bzw. sind Warenzeichen oder eingetragene Warenzeichen der jeweiligen Inhaber. Die Wiedergabe von Marken, Produktnamen, Gebrauchsnamen, Handelsnamen, Warenbezeichnungen u.s.w. in diesem Werk berechtigt auch ohne besondere Kennzeichnung nicht zu der Annahme, dass solche Namen im Sinne der Warenzeichen- und Markenschutzgesetzgebung als frei zu betrachten wären und daher von jedermann benutzt werden dürften.

Bibliographic information published by the Deutsche Nationalbibliothek: The Deutsche Nationalbibliothek lists this publication in the Deutsche Nationalbibliografie; detailed bibliographic data are available in the Internet at http://dnb.d-nb.de.
Any brand names and product names mentioned in this book are subject to trademark, brand or patent protection and are trademarks or registered trademarks of their respective holders. The use of brand names, product names, common names, trade names, product descriptions etc. even without a particular marking in this works is in no way to be construed to mean that such names may be regarded as unrestricted in respect of trademark and brand protection legislation and could thus be used by anyone.

Coverbild / Cover image: www.ingimage.com

Verlag / Publisher:
LAP LAMBERT Academic Publishing
ist ein Imprint der / is a trademark of
OmniScriptum GmbH & Co. KG
Heinrich-Böcking-Str. 6-8, 66121 Saarbrücken, Deutschland / Germany
Email: info@lap-publishing.com

Herstellung: siehe letzte Seite /
Printed at: see last page
ISBN: 978-3-659-58237-0

LAMBERT Academic Publishing

Information systems in education

Ladislav BURITA

2014

Contents

List of figures

4

List of tables

List of abbreviations

1NF	The first Normal Form
2NF	The second Normal Form
3NF	The third Normal Form
ACR	Army of the Czech Republic
BLOB	Binary Large Object
CASE	Computer Aided Software Engineering
CD	Compact Disc
DB	Data Base
DBMS	Data Base Management System
DBS	Data Base System
DD	Data Dictionary
DSS	Decision Support System
DVD	Digital Versatile/Video Disc
EIS	Executive Information System
ERD	Entity Relationship Diagram
FD	Functional Diagram
FEM	Faculty of Economics and Management
FHS	Faculty of Health Sciences
FK	Foreign Key
FMT	Faculty of Military Technology
HW	Hardware
ID	Identifier
IS	Information System

IT	Information Technology
KIMA	Information Management Course for Distance Students
LC	Life Cycle
MIS	Management Information System
MS	Microsoft
MS	Modular Structure
PK	Primary Key
PHP	Personal Home Pages (Hypertext Preprocessor)
RDM	Relational Data Model
RUP	Rational Unified Process
SDM	Software Development Methodology
SSADM	Structured System Analysis and Design Method
SW	Software
TPS	Transaction Processing System
UoD	University of Defence
UTB	University of Tomas Bata in Zlín

Introduction

The publication summarizes expertise and experience of teaching information systems (IS) for more than 25 years. Teaching IS is based on a structured methodology, which is less used in the practice of IS development, but for teaching is very appropriately applied to both Bachelor's level of informatics students and to teach business oriented students (management, economics, entrepreneurship) at the Magister's level. This is confirmed by the results of students work (based on source [3]) and the research in IS education (based on source [2]), presented in the book.

The IS development theme starts with basic concepts explanation and IS modelling in general, followed by structured methodology, complementary by examples. Outcome of the student work is placed in separate chapter, also the result of research of the pedagogic process.

In the studying, analysing, applying, and teaching the IS development was predominantly by author used the sources [8-11]. Many publications about the IS theme were produced, for example [1, 3, 4].

The development of IS for commercial purposes is being executed through agile methodologies and object approaches. Predominantly, web applications are being created, and working with IS by using mobile devices is being solved.

Yet we should not condemn some historical methodology approaches, such as structured methodology; we should use them appropriately with respect to the new conditions, bearing in mind what is important and how they can be useful in teaching. Although the structured methodology is rather historical, its application is still required, e.g. [7].

1 Fundamentals of IS development

This chapter introduces basic concepts of Information Systems (IS), their classification, modelling and development process.

1.1 Basic concepts of IS

The introduction deals with three basic concepts that will be often used: informatization, Information Technology (IT) and Information System (IS).

Informatization means a purposeful process of comprehensive introduction of technological means and design methods into various areas of human activity, enabling an effective use of information while respecting safety and legislative principles, as well as the protection of life, health and human personality. Information is not only an important production tool, but it is also a spiritual base for further development of people in accordance with the laws of nature.

Information Technology refers to the current state of information processing for its wide use in practice. It includes everything that participates in analysis, design, development, implementation and operation of systems for information processing in any way.

The quality and availability of IT mainly depends upon the advances in the following areas:

- Theoretical knowledge in the field of computer science, i.e. the acquisition, processing and utilization of information.
- Technological advances in manufacturing the components ensuring the acquisition, processing and transmission of information (hardware - HW).
- Technological progress in software (SW) development.

Information System includes people, information, information technology, technological means and design methods; a management system running the IS and a system of its work organization. The management system running the IS ensures close and logical connection to the environment, which constitutes a natural framework for the IS, and the system of work organization is associated with the

9

operation and utilization of the IS. Technological means and design methods enable the collection, acquisition, storage, transmission, update, and processing of data with a view to creating and presenting information for the user needs. This set of characteristics of the IS is complemented by the demands on reliability, safety, economic operation and compliance with applicable laws, standards and recommendations.

The aim of the IS is to improve the performance of organizations, to make their activities more effective, to enable high quality and proper decision-making by the management, and to achieve better results (competitiveness). IS can be divided into groups based on various criteria, such as the purpose, size, structural complexity, number and type of users, geographic scope, time characteristics, etc. One of the frequently stated divisions of the IS is based on the relationship of the IS to the organization management, particularly with regard to the position within a level of the information pyramid (see Fig. 1).

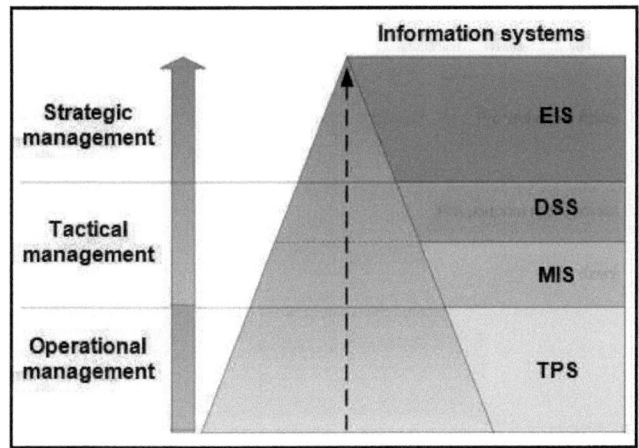

Fig. 1 Information pyramid

There are several types of IS:

- Transaction Processing Systems (TPS);

- Management Information Systems (MIS);

- Decision Support Systems (DSS);

- Executive Information Systems (EIS).

10

The aim of **Transaction Processing Systems** (TPS) is to automate typical business processes, such as calculating payroll, accounting, reservation systems, registration of persons and registration of material. A special case of transactional systems are the **IS for Technological Processes Control.**

Management Information Systems (MIS) produce information reports, selective outputs and summaries based on the data maintained and processed in the TPS, or possibly on the information created by means of the TPS. This information allows managers to monitor and influence the performance of their departments. Typical examples are vrious reports on the plan fulfilment and the economy of individual subjects.

Decision Support Systems (DSS) present, in fact, a natural extension of the MIS. Their aim is to analyze the information, which should assist the managers not only in monitoring and influencing the performance of their departments but also in making vital decisions for the further development of the departments.

Executive Information Systems (EIS) provide managers with information which should assist them in making qualified strategic decisions. EIS integrate the most important data sources of the system (both internal and external) important to the organization control as a whole. EIS provide the selection, aggregation and restructuring of miscellaneous data, particularly from the areas of financial and personnel management, and also from other areas of the organization activities, and offer different views of the data.

1.2 Modelling and IS development

The following sub-chapter deals with the concepts of methodology, method, technique and tool. The approaches and levels of IS modelling are examined here, as well as general principles and modelling procedures.

1.2.1 Methodology, method, technique, tool

The creation and implementation of an IS is a complex and costly activity with a large share of human labour; therefore, it is necessary to approach it systematically. Over the years, a number of different methodologies, the aim of which is to facilitate and standardize the process of IS creation. This development was partly a spontaneous process accompanied by a confusion of concepts. Eventually, the classification of terms has been unified and is being observed – more or less –by all creators and users of IS.

The basic concepts concerning the IS design and development are methodology, methods, technique and tool. These concepts follow a hierarchical structure: from the general concept of methodology to individual tools (see Fig. 2).

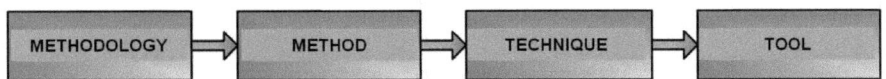

Fig. 2 Concepts: methodology, method, technique, and tool

Methodology is a general guidance for the creation of IS. It covers the entire Life Cycle of the IS creation (or its substantial part). It addresses the **WHY, WHO, WHAT** and **WHEN** questions in the process of the IS creation.

The examples of methodologies are SSADM (Great Britain), MERISE (France), SDM (The Netherlands), V-Methodology (Germany) and the Rational Unified Process (RUP). Each organization developing and implementing IS uses its own methodology based on the general methodological principles and on its own experience.

Method deals with the aspects of an IS development stage; it defines relationships between tools. Each method is burdened with a certain approach, such as functional access, access to data modelling or object-oriented approach. There is a question to be answered: **WHAT** should be done in a particular IS development stage (e.g. in terms of analysis, design and verification, etc.). Some of the well-known methods worth mentioning here are Yourdon Structured Method, Jackson System Development, Marten Information Engineering and object-oriented analysis and design.

Technique consists of fixed procedures – the steps suggesting **HOW** to reach an outcome (e.g. how to create a conceptual view of a system). The examples of techniques are data modelling techniques, data model normalization, and the proposal of a functional structure of the system based on an event method.

Tool is a means expressing an activity outcome carried out by using a particular technique; it is a means that enables using this technique. So the question to be

12

answered is: **WHICH** tool should be used to obtain an outcome? The examples of tools are the Entity-Relationship Diagram, Structural Diagram, Relational Data Model and Use Case.

For the IS support, the specialized software – **CASE** (Computer-Aided Software Engineering) – has been designed. The methodology, methods, techniques and tools are supported by different CASE means (e.g. *ERwin* for entity-relationship and relational modelling; creating the database structure [5]).

1.2.2 Approaches to IS development

When designing an IS, it is possible to apply **approaches** with regard to the facts whether the modelling of the system is based on processes, functions or data. There are two basic groups of approaches: **process-oriented** and **data-oriented**. The approaches of both groups are often combined.

Process-oriented approaches can be either functionally oriented or object-oriented. In case of using the functional approach, the system is modelled as a set of interconnected and cooperating functions. The system is modelled by the means of functions that are linked to data streams. Object-oriented approach models the system as a set of interconnected and cooperating objects. The operations applied to objects are encapsulated within the objects. Data-oriented approach models the basic data structures that can be traced in the system.

1.2.3 IS modelling, models

One of the most important principles of the creation of an IS is modelling. The concept of **model** is here used as a purposefully generated image of the real world (see Fig. 3Fig. 3), which is to be described, analyzed and on the basis of which an IS is to be created. The individual models of reality created by different developers might vary to a large extent, although they are the same part of reality. Therefore, there is a search for methods and procedures of the creation of models that are comprehensive, and thus facilitate understanding between developers and users.

A model is characterized by building blocks – **constructs,** by the means of which the model is created; and by **rules** for using these constructs. In case of graphical models, the graphical signs correspond to constructs-**notation.**

13

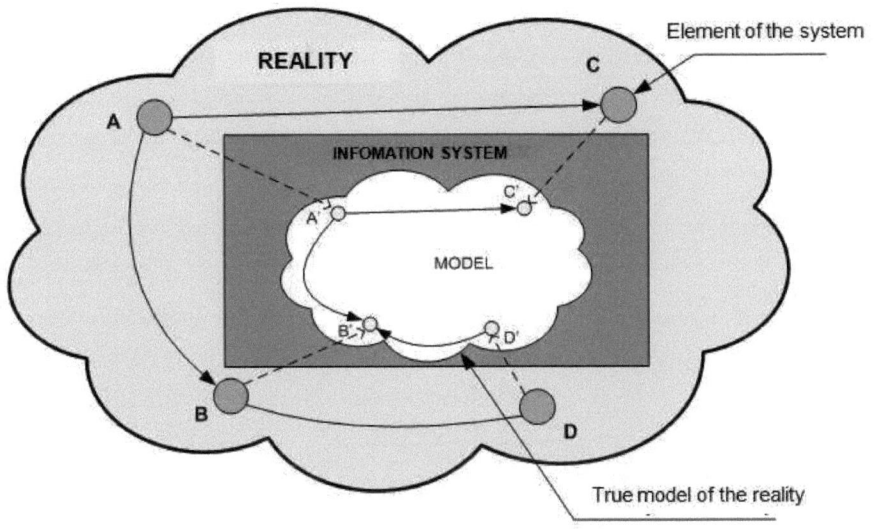

Fig. 3 Model of a part of the real world

A model should meet the following requirements:

- It is concise, clear, in graphic form and accompanied by documentation.
- It allows a hierarchical division of the system.
- It should include minimum redundancy.
- It has to be easily readable and understandable.
- It has to allow the modelling of the system behaviour.
- It is true, formal and accurate.

1.2.4 General principles and procedures in modelling

IS modelling is a complex process. To manage this complexity successfully, it is helpful to apply verified procedures and principles known as **general methods of modelling**. They include, for example, the principles of abstraction, phasing, and the top-down and bottom-up approaches.

The principle of **abstraction** respects our intellectual and thought ability to think within a limited amount of knowledge. Model developers only take into account the essential elements of the reality that is being analyzed and eliminate the elements which are less important. They return to them only after the essential features of the model and its nature have been identified and described.

14

The **phasing** principle leads to the simplification of the complexity of the model creation by dividing it into phases. Each phase focuses on modelling from a certain point of view; it uses its own methods, techniques and tools. For example, the conceptual, logical and physical phase of modelling, or the phases of an IS Life Cycle.

The **structuring** principle identifies the structure of the model by using typical patterns, such as hierarchy or modularity.

Hierarchy is a structure which represents reality at individual levels of detail. The entities belong to a super ordinate entity. The top of the hierarchy is represented by a single entity – a root. For example, the organizational structure of *the University of Defence (UoD)* is shown in Fig. 4 (Rectorate, Faculty of Economics and Management - FEM, Faculty of Military Technology - FMT, Faculty of Health Sciences - FHS).

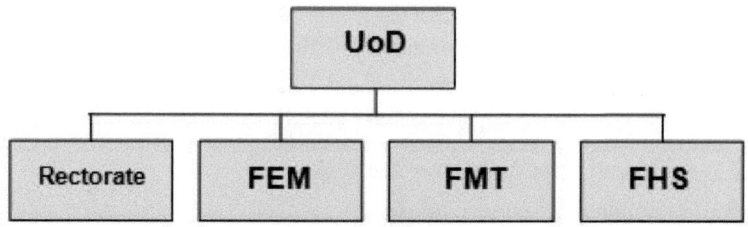

Fig. 4 Faculties of the University of Defence

Modular structure is not constructed on the basis of the principles of unequivocal superiority or subordination; the individual components – modules – can be interconnected arbitrarily. An example is a modular structure of an application program in Fig. 5.

Top-down approach is used by model creators when the modelled reality as a whole (system) is taken into account at first; then its individual components (sub-systems) are gradually distinguished, and after that the further detailed parts in them… until there is the last distinguishing level of the individual elements of the model (system).

Bottom-up approach is used by model creators who first focus on individual elements of the modelled reality; gradually, they combine the elements to create sub-units… to sub-systems, which are put together to create the structure of the model (system).

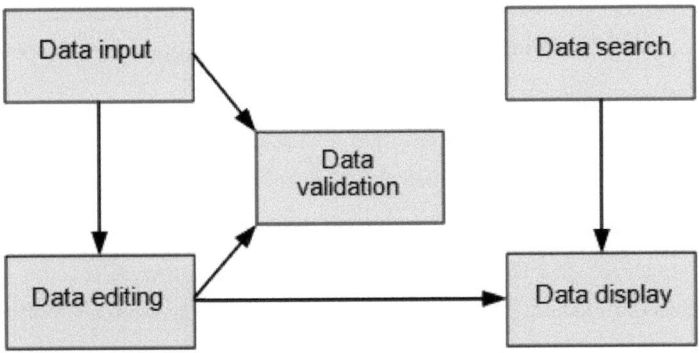

Fig. 5 Modular structure of application program

1.2.5 IS Life Cycle and its documentation

IS development, as well as many other large-scale activities in any field of human activity, is carried out through a *project*. An IS passes through certain stages from its beginning to its end, which is referred to as the IS Life Cycle (LC). The concept of **project** includes the process of planning and managing large-scale operations. With regard to the general and diverse nature of projects, the concept of project is not easy to be defined, so it useful to state its characteristics:

- Time limit (temporality, start, end).

- Clearly defined objectives (including the requirement for the quality).

- Working process leading towards achieving the objectives.

- Uniqueness, non-cyclicity, vastness, diversity and complexity.

- Limited resources, uncertainty and degree of risk.

- United effort of experts of different expertise (synergy of their activities).

Each project is accompanied by a number of organizational, personnel, financial, technical, programming, building, technological, safety and operational (sometimes even by more) measures and activities.

IS Life Cycle is a concept closely connected to the access to the IS creation and methodology. The interpretation of the LC in this chapter is predominantly tied to a structured approach and conveys a certain tradition in the field of IS.

LC stands for a process of collecting and analyzing the requirements for the future IS: the design process, building procedure, implementation, operation, improvement or possible abolition of the IS.

An IS LC often starts with not entirely accurate ideas about the objectives and benefits for the client, and ends when the project becomes obsolete and inapplicable with regard to the IS operation.

Completed stages of the IS development and operation are called the **Life Cycle phases**. Within the phases, the steps that have to be accomplished are defined.

The research team applies one of the methodologies; this should be certainly approached in a creative way with regard to specific circumstances. Therefore, the classification of the IS LC types of is rather a theoretical issue. In practice, the project solution often includes different combinations of LC types.

1.2.6 Waterfall - sequential life cycle of IS development

An example of the LC phases is the waterfall or sequential methodology. Each phase follows its predecessor and must be completely finished, when the next phase starts.

Pre-project preparation

Stemming from the project requirements, the objective of this phase is to prepare a **work schedule for the IS development** *and* an **initial study.** The work schedule addresses the basic issues associated with managing the project, e.g. the optimization design of all resources – people, time, financial, technical and software resources. The initial study mainly elaborates the requirements and addresses the expected consequences of the IS implementation into the organization. In this phase, management should introduce appropriate measures prior to IS implementation.

Analysis

Analysis leads to the development of precise **specifications of the IS** based on the customer requirements, plans and objectives, clarified in the pre-project preparation phase, and a collection of user demands.

Design

In this phase, the whole IS is designed. For the sake of clarity, the design is usually

17

created in two steps as a **global** *and* **detailed** design. Within the global design step (architectural design), the system in focus is divided into sub-systems, which can be separately implemented, tested and verified in a trial operation. Within the detailed design step, the global design is refined to a level at which it is possible to begin the implementation of individual components of sub-systems (modules).

Implementation

The aim of this phase is to **create** a **functioning system.** This includes the development, testing and trial operation of the new system.

Deployment

The **IS is put into operation**; the **routine operation starts**.

Operation and maintenance

The aim is to ensure smooth operation of the system under both normal and emergency conditions, and ensure that the system always satisfies the requirements set down by the organization. In this phase, the periodic assessment of the current IS is carried out, and recommendations for its further development are made.

1.3 Review of a project

Each phase (except the operation and maintenance stages) should end with a **peer review session**. It serves as a legislative basis for the approval of the outcomes of the ongoing project and for assigning further work on the project, or a significant change in the project requirements or even a complete cessation of the project. A peer review session is organized by the stakeholder who also appoints a peer review committee. The participants of peer review sessions are:

- a peer review committee (chairman, secretary and members);
- peer reviewers;
- invited participants (representatives of users, independent experts);
- members of the research team.

Materials for the peer review session are sent by the organizer in cooperation with the research team to the participants of the session, so that they received them in time, prior to the peer review session. A **peer reviewer** is an independent person whose opinion cannot be considered the opinion of the organization he or she works for. Only the peer review committee members possess the voting right.

The agenda of the peer review session usually includes:

- opening (chairman);

- stating project requirements (stakeholder);

- status of achievements (team leader);

- presentation of peer reviewers' opinions;

- defence of the project solution (team leader);

- discussion (all participants);

- resolution processing and its approval (peer review committee);

- announcement of the conclusion. (peer review committee chairman).

The peer review session is recorded in the resolution protocol and minutes. The resolution assesses whether the project requirements have been met, and provides the conclusions of the reviewers' opinions and results of the vote. The minutes include the objective of the session, date and place, list of participants, agenda of the session and suggestions made by the participants. The reviewers' opinions and researchers' defence and other important documents are included.

2 Structured methodology

This chapter explains a **structured approach** to the modelling of reality and creation of an Information System (IS), its levels and dimensions. The chapter introduces the tools and techniques of data and functional modelling. Particular attention is paid to the Entity Relationship Diagram (ERD) and the Relational Data Model (RDM). The theory is illustrated by examples, facilitating the understanding of the topic.

2.1 Fundamentals of a structured approach

The modelling of reality aims to describe the reality in an Information System as accurately as possible. By using a structured approach or structured methodology, the reality is modelled by the means of three elements (dimensions): ***data, functions*** and ***events,*** see Fig. 6.

Data describe real and abstract objects such as persons, CDs, ideas...

Functions describe the processes and actions performed by the objects. Functions normally lead to data transformation, such as "recording personal data of a person just starting a job", "creating a timetable for a semester", and "borrowing a CD".

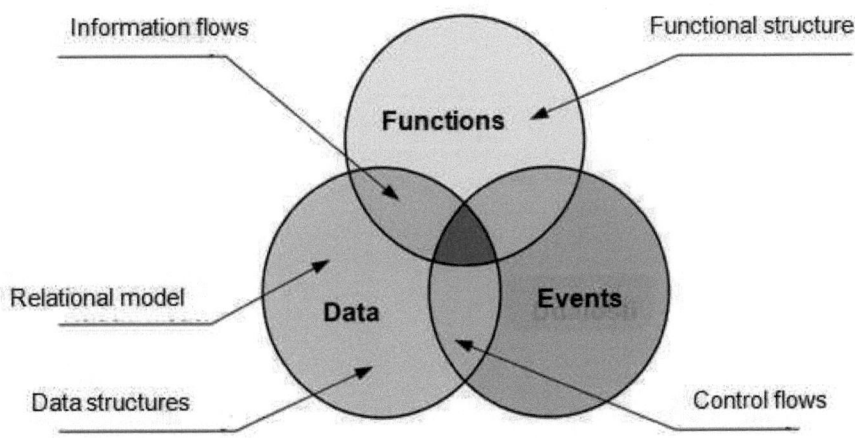

Fig. 6 Modelling dimensions

20

Events are actions in reality demanding a response in the IS, such as "starting a job", "a new semester at school", "purchasing a CD for a library", "origin of an idea", ...

Structured approach to modelling involves the **conceptual, logical** and **physical** levels (see Fig. 7).

Conceptual level requires the most accurate description of reality regardless of the technological environment in which it takes place.

Logical level is based on the conceptual model and takes into account the future technological environment.

Physical level is based on the logical model; application programs in the development environment are created and the structure of the database is defined.

Each level of modelling is represented by several models. They serve as examples of possible choices of models; the other ways of the IS creation are possible.

The **conceptual level** includes:

- **ERD** – Entity Relationship Diagram;
- **DD** – Data Dictionary;
- **FD** – Functional Diagram.

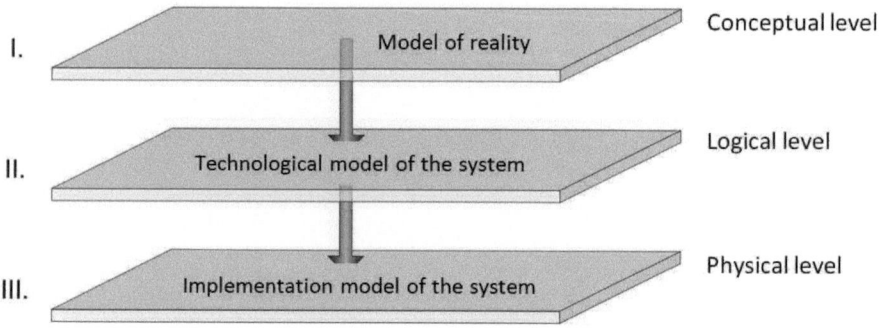

Fig. 7 Three levels of IS modelling

The **logical level** includes:

- **RDM** – Relational Data Model;
- **DD** – Data Dictionary;
- **MS** – Modular Structure.

The **physical level** includes:

- **DB schema** defined from DD;
- **DB** (Data Base);
- **Applications** in the selected Data Base Management System (DBMS).

Each model is briefly characterized and model **constructs** (elements of which the model is formed) and the **rules** for the model creation are described. Finally, an example of the model described is given. In this chapter, the data view is favoured (the crucial factor is data modelling).

The constructs occur in two forms in modelling. In an **abstract** (or **definition**) form, is represented by common names standing for a particular group. For example, the entity "PERSON" includes all persons. Such an abstract concept is referred to as a **type.** The second case is about a specific form of the entity – **occurrence**. For example: a person "Charles ONDRYHAL".

2.2 An example – requirements specification

The explanation of methodology is accompanied by an illustrative example, which is also going to be integrated into the IS Life Cycle phases and levels of modelling. In the preparatory phase, the **requirements** for the intended IS are specified. The demands on the IS are identified, available information about the organization in focus is gathered and studied, necessary costs and potential benefits are estimated and potential risks are stated.

Generally, **the preparatory phase** focuses on:
- Identification of shortcomings in the run of the organization, the specification of problems and the assessment of the state of the information available.
- The assessment of whether the analysed processes are suitable for automation.

22

- Setting objectives for the IS creation, development and innovation.
- Costs, expected benefits and risks estimate.
- Project requirements specification.

Example of IS

Create an "Information system on companies which sell software products and hardware components" for the Computer Technology Acquisition Department. Record of SW products, HW components and suppliers; record data about the companies and the important HW and SW parameters, including cost.
The requirements for processing the data concerning the companies:
- *Inserting, updating and deleting (name, address, contact details ...).*
- *Searching an appropriate company and creating reports.*

Requirements for processing the data on software (SW) and hardware (HW):
- *Inserting, updating and deleting (title, author, platform type, cost ...).*
- *Searching a suitable product.*
- *Working with the price list.*

A survey on the requirements for the IS can be prepared in the form of a questionnaire, as shown in Tab. 1.

Requirements specification

The information system will process data on companies, software products and hardware components. It should allow recording, updating, data searching and creating information reports. Information processing has to be ensured both in details, and in the reciprocal context (e.g. company – product). All versions of the updated price lists of the products of the companies have to be accessible during a course of time.

This instance is suitable for automation; in the case of large scale companies and numerous products, it can considerably save time and financial resources. IS should store and process information on the companies and their products or components which are produced or distributed. It is necessary to enable the following functions:

- Inserting a new company, including several addresses for one company.
- Editing, deleting and searching companies.
- Providing SW products and HW components in relation to the company.

Our progression to the IS on Companies-SW-HW proceeds with the ERD design. In the first approach, the outcomes of the analysis of the subject area are three entities: COMPANY, HW and SW with corresponding relationships (see Fig. 8). For the time being, let us disregard the characteristics of entities. In the second approach to the reality in the ERD, we intend to discuss in detail the entities COMPANY and SW (the part with HW entity is analogous) (see Fig. 9). Regarding the analysed reality and assignment requirements, the SW has to be considered as a SWPRODUCT, which operates within an environment of a certain platform (SWPLATFORM) and belongs to a group of software (SWTYPE). We consider the location of the company at the address/addresses (ADDRESS).

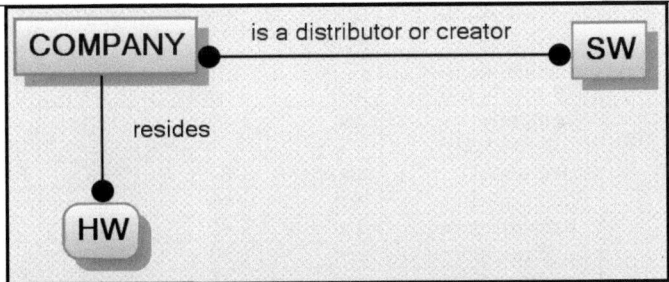

Fig. 8 ERD – first approach (COMPANY – SW – HW)

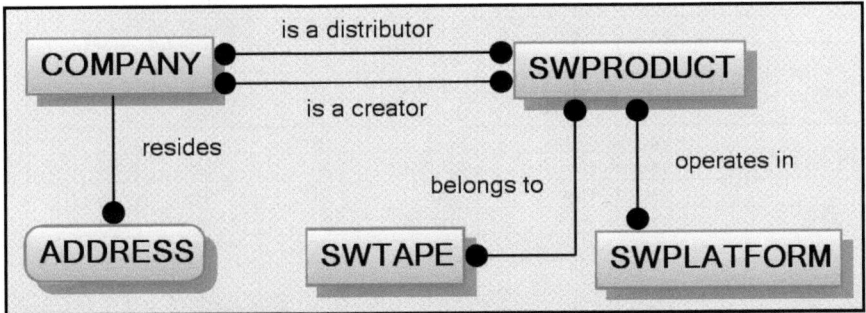

Fig. 9 ERD in detail for COMPANY – SW

2.3.2 Data Dictionary

Data Dictionary (DD) accompanies the entire IS Life Cycle from the IS requirements specification, through analysis, design, development, implementation and operation. DD contains general description of the data about data – **metadata,** representing the reality, which will be maintained later in the database (DB). DB is the centre of the IS, which is crucial to architects, developers and managers of IS as well as to SW applications for data processing.

Example data dictionary

Our progression to the information system on companies, SW and HW proceeds with the Data Dictionary design (see Tab. 4) related to the ERD specified in Fig. 9.

Tab. 4 Data Dictionary as an illustrative example

Entity	Attribute	Data type	Length	Obli-gation	Primary key
COMPANY	company-ID	number	5	Yes	PK
	company-name	text	60	Yes	
	company-foundation date	date			
	company-profile	text	note		
	company-representative	text	100		
ADDRESS	address-ID	number	5	Yes	PK
	address-city	text	40	Yes	
	address-street	text	40	Yes	
	address-phone	text	30	Yes	
	address-Email	text	15	Yes	
	address-contact	text	note	Yes	
SW PRODUCT	swprod-ID	number	5	Yes	PK
	swprod-name	text	200	Yes	
	swprod-version	text	20		
	swprod-price	number	18	Yes	
	swprod-date	date		Yes	
	swprod-note	text	note		
SW PLATFORM	swplatf-ID	number	5	Yes	PK
	swplatf-name	text	200	Yes	
SW TYPE	swtype-ID	number	5	Yes	PK
	swtype-name	text	200	Yes	

2.3.3 Functional Diagram

Functional Diagram (FD), as a model of conceptual level of modelling, represents the first account of functional possibilities of the future IS. The base for the FD design is an ERD, from the entities of which the functions are derived. The construct of the FD is a **structural diagram** composed of blocks (also a block diagram). Types of blocks are shown in Tab. 5.

An example of a structural diagram is shown in Fig. 10, where the DIAGRAM is made up of sequences of blocks A + B + C; block A consists of a sequence of blocks

29

A1 + A2 + A3, block B is the block BI **iteration** in line with *condB,* and block C a **selection** of blocks C1, C2, C3 in line with *condC.*

Tab. 5 Structural blocks

Block type	Diagram	Explanation
sequence		Sequential blocks describe activities that are processed in sequence following the diagram
iteration (cycle)	cycle condition *	Iteration block is repeatedly processed in line with the cycle condition
selection	selection condition O	Selection block is processed in line with the selection condition

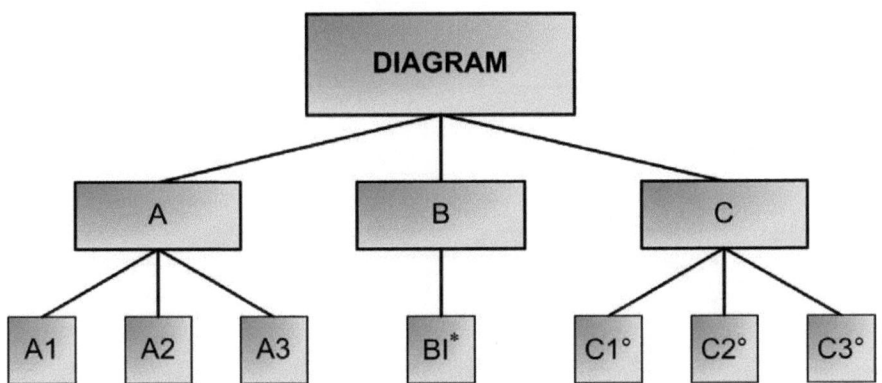

Fig. 10 Structural diagram

When creating a functional diagram, two approaches can be applied:

1. **Object approach** – the ERD objects are the starting point (see Fig. 11) and the technological steps are assigned to them.

2. **System approach** – the technological steps are the starting point (see Fig. 12) and the ERD objects are assigned to them.

Example

30

Our progression to the information system on companies, SW and HW proceeds with a Functional Diagram design – an object approach (see Fig. 11) and system approach (see Fig. 12).

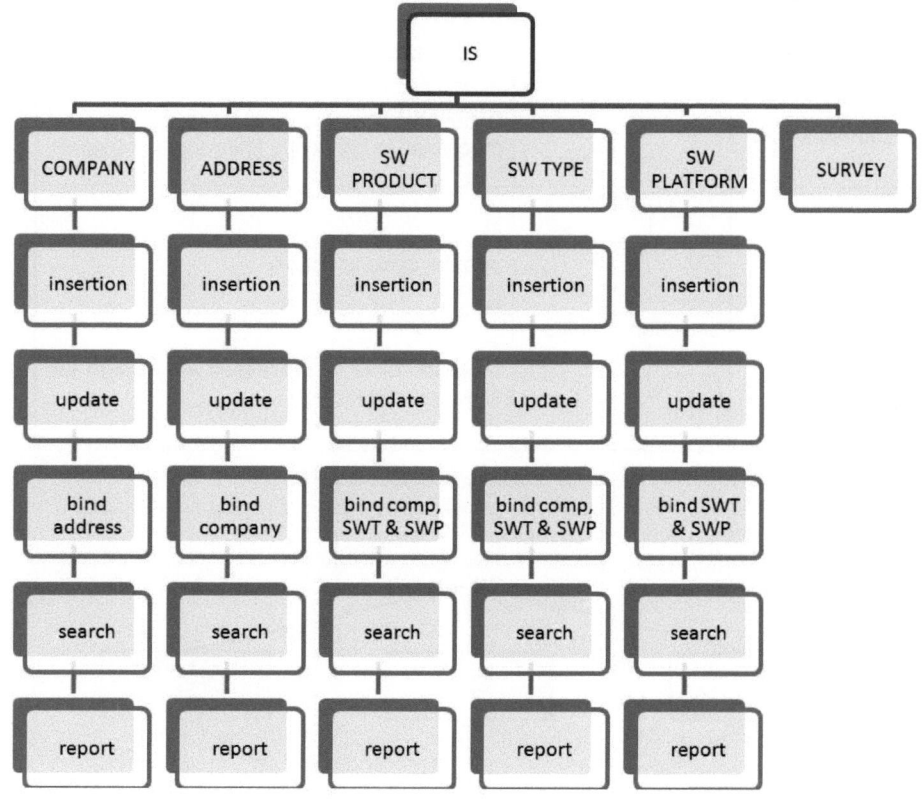

Fig. 11 Functional Diagram – an object approach

2.4 Logical level of modelling

The logical level of modelling makes possible the creation of the reality models that respect the possibilities and requirements of the technological environment of the future IS, and, at the same time, they are based on the conceptual level models.

The following sub-chapters examine Relational Data Model (RDM), Data Dictionary (DD), and Modular Structure (MS).

31

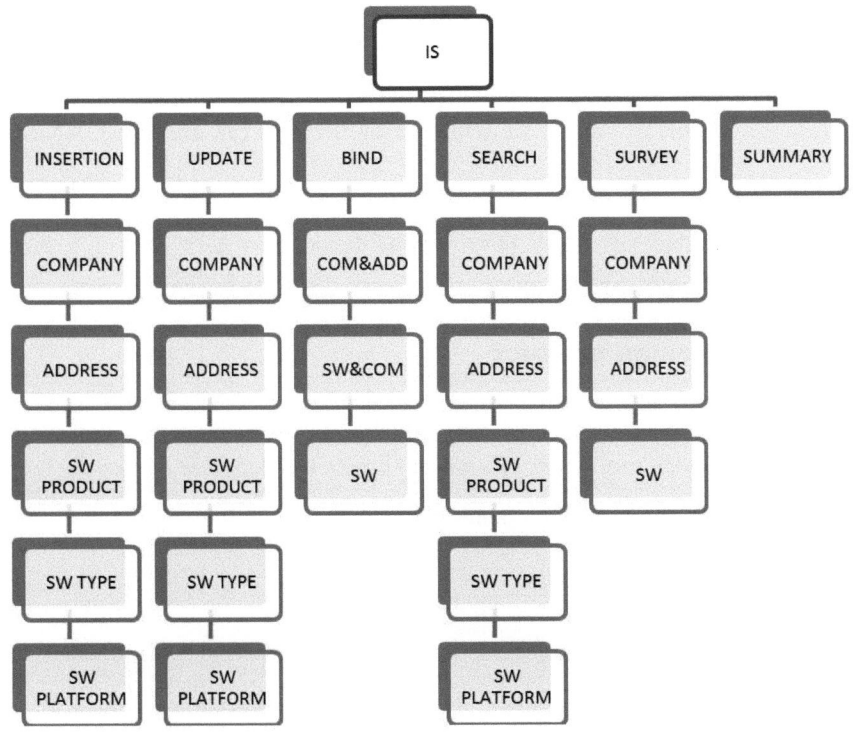

Fig. 12 Functional Diagram – a system approach

2.4.1 Relational Data Model

According to its author E. F. Codd (1971), RDM is a table view of data and is more acceptable to users than other to date structures [6]. The database in the RDM is mathematically defined and is independent of computer implementation. The table in the RDM respects the following properties.

1. Homogeneity of columns (the same data type in the column).

2. The columns are named.

3. At the intersection of a row and column of the table is a simple data field.

4. The row is identified by an unambiguous value of one or more of the columns.

5. The order of the rows and columns does not matter.

6. There are no equal rows and columns.

RDM definition

Let us consider a non-empty set of elements of A_1, A_2, ..., A_n (n>=1), called attributes. Let a tuple of values is a sequence of elements $(a_1, a_2, ..., a_n)$, where $a_1 \in A_1$, $a_2 \in A_2$, ..., $a_n \in A_n$.

The Cartesian product of sets A_i (1=< i <=n) denote $S = A_1 \times A_2 \times ... \times A_n$. The **relation R** of the degree **N** is a subset of **S**, **R** $\subset$ **S**, denote **R** $(A_1, A_2, ... ,A_n)$.

Example Cartesian product

*Let us consider a nonempty set of elements of A_1, A_2, A_3, where $A_1=(a,b,c)$, $A_2=(0,1)$, $A_3=(x,y)$. The Cartesian product $R=A_1 \times A_2 \times A_3$ is the matrix of values (combinations 3x2x2=12 of elements), see **Tab. 6**. The relation can be any subset of **S**, such as Tab. 7.*

Tab. 6 Relation R, the Cartesian product

a	0	x
b	0	x
c	0	x
a	1	x
b	1	x
c	1	x
a	0	y
b	0	y
c	0	y
a	1	y
b	1	y
c	1	y

Tab. 7 Example of relation S, as a subset of relation R

c	0	y
a	1	y
b	1	y
c	1	y

2.4.2 Transformation of the ERD to RDM

The transformation of the ERD to RDM lies in converting their corresponding constructs. An entity will convert to a table and an attribute to a table column. A relationship in the ERD does not have an equivalent in the RDM, therefore it has to be replaced in a way, which ensures that the information obtained in the data will not be lost when analysing the environment (the content of the data model must not be changed).

The transformation of the cardinality relationships of 1:1 and 1:N is carried out by inserting a Foreign Key (FK) into the child table in a relationship. The foreign key are the primary key attributes in the parent table in the relationship, see Fig. 13.

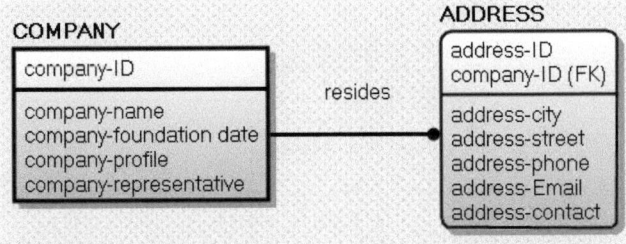

Fig. 13 Transformation of a relationships of 1:1 and 1:N

Fig. 14 The relationship M:N before transformation

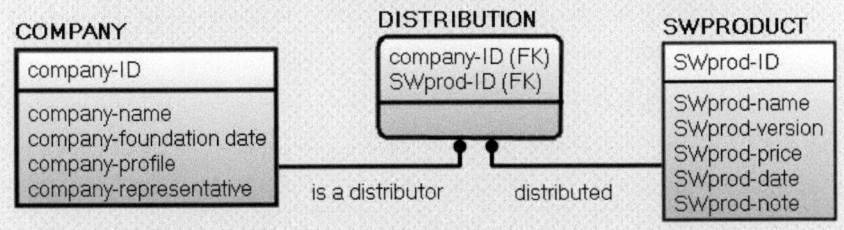

Fig. 15 The relationship M:N after transformation

The transformation of unspecified relationships of M:N is carried out by inserting a Relation Table, into which the primary keys from both entities migrate; see Fig. 14 (before transformation) and Fig. 15 (after transformation). By inserting the relational table the relation M:N divides into two cardinality relations 1:N.

34

Example complete ERD

Our progression to the IS COMPANY-SW proceeds with a RDM design, more precisely with the ERD transformation following the representation in Fig. 9 and the DD designed to a RDM in Tab. 8; see a key level picture in Fig. 16.

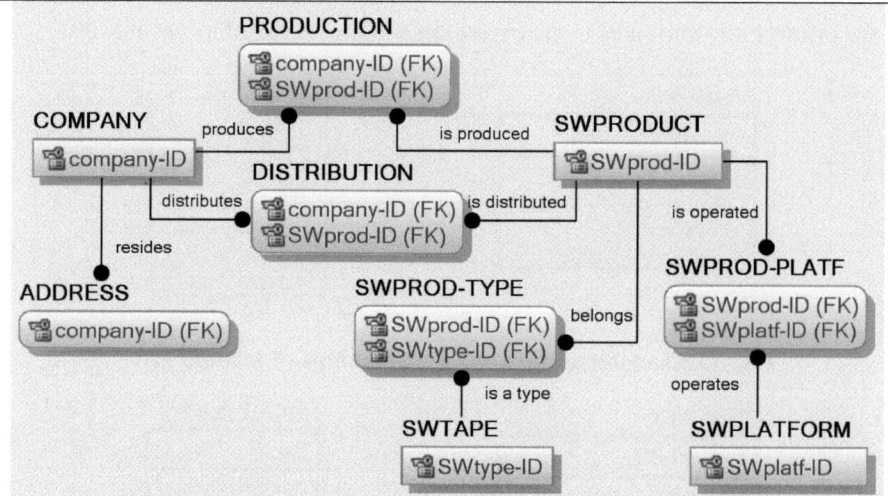

Fig. 16 Relational Data Model COMPANY – SW (only key level)

2.4.3 Data Dictionary

DD based on the logical level of modelling moves from the conceptual level, and then it is complemented with regard to the RDM. It mainly concerns the newly created tables (relational tables) and specification of their content.

Example DD for RDM

Complete the data dictionary from the conceptual level of modelling (see Tab. 4) with regard to the RDM specified in Fig. 16. The result is given in Tab. 8.

2.4.4 Normalization of the RDM

The RDM was obtained by the transformation of the ERD. The question is whether the proposed relations (tables) are optimized in terms of data processing. What can cause problems are the relationships between attributes (columns of the table). The process by means of which the unwanted relationships are removed, but at the same time the content of the model remains unreduced (without the loss of information

35

value) is called **normalization**. Normalization leads to the substitution of the set of tables by another set of tables whose structure is easier and more appropriate for the operations of inserting, updating and deleting data and restructuring tables.

Tab. 8 Data dictionary for an exemplary example (logical level)

Table	Column	Data type	Length	Oblig ation	Prim-key
COMPANY	company-ID	number	5	Yes	PK
	company-name	text	60	Yes	
	company-foundation date	date			
	company-profile	text	note		
	company-representative	text	100		
ADDRESS	address-ID	number	5	Yes	PK
	company-ID	number	5	Yes	FK
	address-city	text	40	Yes	
	address-street	text	40	Yes	
	address-phone	text	30	Yes	
	address-Email	text	15	Yes	
	address-contact	text	note	Yes	
SWPRODUCT	SWprod-ID	number	5	Yes	PK
	SWprod-name	text	200	Yes	
	SWprod-version	text	20		
	SWprod-price	number	18	Yes	
	SWprod-date	date		Yes	
	SWprod-note	text	Note		
SWPLATFORM	SWplatf-ID	number	5	Yes	PK
	SWplatf-name	text	200	Yes	
SWTYPE	SWtype-ID	number	5	Yes	PK
	SWtype-name	text	200	Yes	
SWPROD-PLATF	SWprod-ID	number	5	Yes	FK
	SWplatf-ID	number	5	Yes	FK
SWPROD-TYPE	SWprod-ID	number	5	Yes	FK
	SWplatf-ID	number	5	Yes	FK
PRODUCTION	company-ID	number	5	Yes	FK
	SWprod-ID	number	5	Yes	FK
DISTRIBUTION	company-ID	number	5	Yes	FK
	SWprod-ID	number	5	Yes	FK

The process of normalization will gradually convert the set of tables to the first (1NF), the second (2NF) and the third normal form (3NF). There are also other normal forms; however, they are rarely applied in practice, therefore they are not included.

The table is:

1. In 1NF if it does not contain repeating columns. Multiple columns are placed in a separate table.
2. In 2NF if it is already in 1NF and all non-key columns are fully dependent on the primary key. The columns that are not dependent on the key are placed in a separate table.
3. In 3NF if it is already in 2NF and there are no functional dependencies (relationships) among the non-key columns. The columns that have functional dependencies are placed in a separate table.

Example 1NF

Let us consider a relation PERSON (P-ID, P-surname, ..., P-child1, P-child2...). The P-children is a repeated attribute (a person may have none, one or more children), see Tab. 9. Convert the relation PERSON into the 1NF. The outcomes are in Tab. 10.

Tab. 9 Unnormalized relation PERSON

PERSON (P-ID, P-surname, ... ,P-child1, P-child2, ...)		
211	Pannalis	
213	Nowak	Peter, Magdalene
314	Mister	Jane
413	Dragon	David

Tab. 10 Relations in 1NF (PERSON1 and CHILD)

PERSON1 (P-ID, P-surname, ...)		CHILD (C-ID,	P-ID,	P-child, ...)
211	Pannalis	10	213	Peter
213	Nowak	11	213	Magdalene
314	Mister	12	314	Jane
413	Dragon	13	413	David

Example 2NF

Let us consider a relation MATERIAL (M-ID, M-depot, M-name, M-quantity, D-place, D-name), see

Tab. 11, which is in 1NF but not in 2NF, since not all attributes are dependent on the primary key. Convert the relation to 2NF. See the result in Tab. 12.

Explanation:

M-ID (identification of the material), M-depot (identification of the depot), M-name (name of material), M-quantity (number of pieces), D-place (depot location), D-name (depot name).

Remarks:

M-name depends only on the M-ID; M-quantity depends only on the M-ID;

D-place depends only on the M-depot; D-name depends only on the M-depot.

Tab. 11 Relation MATERIAL in 1NF

MATERIAL (M-ID,	M-depot,	M-name,	M-quantity,	D-place,	D-name)
211	21	Shoes 62	12000	Prague	Clothing
213	11	Subm-gun 72	1000	Brno	Ordnance
314	21	Cap 62	12000	Prague	Clothing
413	11	Pistol 99	500	Brno	Ordnance

Tab. 12 Relations MATERIAL1 and DEPOT in 2NF

MATERIAL1 (M-ID,	M-depot,	M-name,	M-quantity)
211	21	Shoes 62	12000
213	11	Submachine gun 72	1000
314	21	Cap 62	12000
413	11	Pistol 99	500

DEPOT (M-depot,	D-place,	D-name)
21	Prague	Clothing
11	Brno	Ordnance

Example 3NF

Let us consider a relation PERSON-FC (P-item, P-surname, …, P-posit, P-depart, ..., P-workpl), see

Tab. 13, which is in 2NF but not in 3NF, as there are attributes (P-department and P-workplace), which are mutually dependent. Convert the relation to 3NF. See the outcome in Tab. 14.

Tab. 13 Relation PERSONP in 2NF

PERSON-FC (P-ID,	P-surname, …,	P-posit,	P-depart, …	, P-workpl)
211	Kodas	ASSIST	ISgroup	KS-B3-204
213	Nowak	SECR	Manag	KS-B3-101
314	Mister	ASSIST	PRgroup	KS-B3-207
413	Dragon	HEAD	ISgroup	KS-B3-204

Tab. 14 Relations PERSONP1 and PLACEMENT in 3NF

PERSON-FC1 (P-ID,	P-surname,	P-posit,	P-depart)
211	Kodas	ASSIST	ISgroup
213	Nowak	SECR	Manag
314	Mister	ASSIST	PRgroup
413	Dragon	HEAD	ISgroup

PLACEMENT (P-depart,	P-workpl)
ISgroup	KS-B3-204

Manag	KS-B3-101
PRgroup	KS-B3-207

2.4.5 Relational operations

RDM has two aspects: 1) **definition**, associated with relations and 2) **manipulation**, concerning operations of relations. The mathematical basis of the RDM is set theory, so the operations with relations are the operations with sets referred to as **relational algebra**.

Predominantly, in relational algebra normal set operations can be performed, such as union, intersection, difference and Cartesian product. However, the typical operations of relational algebra are **projection** (selection of columns of the relation or limitation of the relation), **restriction** (selection of rows of the relation or filtration), **and union** (union of relations) and **join** (join of relations).

Relational operations of projection and restrictions are **unary operations** (one relation on the input of the operation results in one relation on the output). Relational union and join operations are **binary operations** (two relations on the input of the operation result in one relation on the output). In the relational union operation the input relation has to be **compatible** (comparable in terms of columns and their types), and in the relational join operation there has to be a **compatible attribute of joining** both relations.

Definition of the projection operation

Let us consider a relation $R(A_1, A_2, ... ,A_n)$, from which we want to select a subset of attributes **B**. The result of the projection operation of the set of attributes B in the relation R is the relation R_p, which is defined as **PROJ [R(A), B] = R_p.**

Example projection

Let $R(A_1, A_2, ... ,A_5)$ be a relation and $B = (A_1, A_2, A_5)$ a selected set of attributes .
The projection of the selected set of attributes **B** in relation **R** is $R_p(A_1, A_2, A_5)$.

Definition of the restriction operation

Let us consider a relation $R(A_1, A_2, \ldots, A_n)$, from which we want to choose a set of rows (perform filtering or selection of the relation), whose attributes A_i ($1 =< i <= n$) satisfy the relation V_i (operation $=, <>, >, <, >=, <=$), to the values of H_i.

The restriction operation is written as $\textbf{RESTR [R(A), V_i H_i] = R_r(A)}$.

Example restriction

*Let **PERSON (P-ID, P-surname, F-code)** be a relation from which we want to select all persons (the rows of the PERSON relation) with a function code F-code = 110 (Head of Department). It results in the relation*
PERSON110 = RESTR [PERSON (P-ID, P-surname, F-code), F-code=110].

Definition of the union operation

Let a relation $R(A_1, A_2, \ldots, A_n)$ with rows **a** and a relation $S(B_1, B_2, \ldots, B_k)$ with rows **b** be compatible relations (n=k; relevant columns are the same data type). Then the union operation of the relations **R** and **S** is the operation $\textbf{T = R} \cup \textbf{S}$, which we write as **UNION [R, S] = T**, where $T(C_1, C_2, \ldots, C_n)$ has attributes compatible with **R(A)** a **R(B)** and rows **a + b**.

Note: The result is a relation that has the same number of columns as R (and as S), and contains the rows of relation R and rows of relation S.

Example union

*Let **FUNCTION_K (F-code, F-name)** be a relation which describes the positions of the faculty departments, and **FUNCTION_D (F-code, F-name)** be a relation describing the functions of the faculty Dean's Office. Create a relation with all functions at the faculty. It results in the relation **FUNCTION_F (F-code, F-name)** arising from the union operation of the relations **FUNCTION_K** and **FUNCTION_D**.*

Definition of the join operation

Let A_i be an attribute of a relation $R(A_1, A_2, \ldots, A_n)$ and B_j an attribute of $S(B_1, B_2, \ldots, B_m)$; A_i and B_j are compatible. The join operation of the relation **R** according to the attribute A_i with relation **S** according to the attribute B_j is a binary relational operation, the resulting relation of which is

$$R[A_i = B_j]S = \{(a,b) \mid a \in R, b \in S, (a [A_i] = b[B_j]\},$$

where **a, b** are the rows of the corresponding relations.

Note:

The join operation results in a relation with chain rows of both relations under the fulfilled condition: $A_i = B_j$. It is called a *natural join*.

Example join

Let **PERSON (*P-ID*, P-surname, F-code)** be a relation of the school staff and let the relation **POSITION (*F-code*, F-name)** describe the positions of the school staff (Tab. 15). Create a list of the employees and their positions (surnames of the employees and their positions). First, let us carry out the join operation between relations PERSON and POSITION through the F-code attribute. It results in the relation PERSONP. Finally, by the projection of the relation PERSONP the required list is obtained; see Tab. 16, where the list is still in alphabetical order.

Tab. 15 Relation PERSON and POSITION

PERSON (P-ID, P-surname, F-code)			POSITION (F-code, F-name)	
211	Pannalis	104	102	Secretary
213	Nowak	102	103	HEAD
314	Mister	104	104	Assistent
413	Dragon	103		

Tab. 16 Join operation and list of persons

PERSONP (P-ID, P-surname, F-code, F-name)				LIST OF PERSONS	
211	Pannalis	104	Assistent	Dragon	HEAD
213	Nowak	102	Secretary	Pannalis	Assistent
314	Mister	104	Assistent	Mister	Assistent
413	Dragon	103	HEAD	Nowak	Secretary

2.4.6 Modular structure

Modular structure is created by further elaboration on the FD (Fig. 11 and Fig. 12) into more details prior to the actual creation of the application.

2.5 Physical level of modelling

At the physical level of modelling the actual IS is developed. This includes the creation of the database schema in the selected DBMS, which is, in most cases (if SW for the automated design support is used for data modelling) possible to accomplish by generating from the logical data model. In other cases is the proper DD the source of the scheme definition.

Then we work on software based on the modular structure, utilizing the development environment of the selected DBMS. After that we fill in the DB by means of the part of the application created for inserting the data into the DB. Finally, the resulting IS is subject to testing and can be run.

We used in the education DBMS Microsoft (MS) Access that is simple enough, but useful for the IS creation at the professional basis. We recommend to obtain the needed documentation of the actual version of MS Access and work on the own IS independently.

3 Example of IS, developed by student

The example is a result of the course "IS development" at the Bachelor's level for informatics oriented students at the Faculty of Military Technology, University of Defence, Brno, Czech Republic. First is explained the structure and content of the course; motivational aspects are mentioned and the IS development is described. Source of the chapter is in the conference paper [3].

3.1 Structure and content of the course

The course begins with the analysis of IS issues. It includes the following topics: the concept of IS, its meaning and classification, data - information – knowledge, database system (DBS), data structures of DBS, the function of DBMS and DB properties. Then follows the teaching of the IS modelling. It includes the topics of the IS model, general principles of modelling, IS life cycle, methodology - method - technique - tool.

After that a structured approach to IS development and a conceptual level of modelling are introduced. This part can be described as the core for understanding the field and the proper basis for analytical thinking of an IS creator. The structured methodology (levels and dimensions of modelling, application of approaches to modelling, a conceptual level model) are explained. The constructs and rules of the ERD, FD, and DD are presented.

The course also includes the creation of IS by students themselves. The necessary information is conveyed through an example, starting with the specifications and finding requirements for the IS, proceeding to various levels of modelling, creating the custom application and documenting the process and outcome. The theme for the creation of an IS is chosen by the students themselves. The procedure for the IS development and the outcome are given by detailed guidelines.

In the last part of the course, the logical and physical levels of IS modelling are introduced. They include the RDM, the transformation of the ERD to RDM, RDM normalization, and relational operations. The development environment is MS Access and the description of the basic elements of the application are presented.

In the case of the 'business' oriented students, some of the passages can be omitted or modified, and thus the learning objectives can be adapted to the students' needs. It is not necessary to present the details of DBS, it is possible to replace the definition of the RDM by the 'table view of data', to omit normalization and relational operations. In addition, this group of students could become more familiar with the work in MS Access. The course requirements include a course credit and an examination. The credit is earned for developing and documenting an IS.

3.2 Motivational aspects of the course

The basic motivational tool is continuous repetition of the teaching content and checking the students' skills and knowledge by testing them. Their test results are part of their final evaluation. In addition, the process of the IS creation is checked individually, the ERD design and its transformation into the RDM are discusses.

A well-proven motivational tool is the choice of the IS theme according to student's interest. It is easier to design and create an IS when the student is familiar with its environment and has a positive relationship with it. After several years of assigning this task, it can be summarized that the most popular topics for IS creations are:

- ICT (computers, graphic cards, mobile phones, software, data media, satellite communication, errors of security codes, overview on signals).
- Trade and services (car / motorcycle sales or service, mobile phones)
- Music (music bands and singers, DVD, musical instruments).
- Sports competition (soccer, fire sports, athletics, shooting, body building).
- Teaching (student records, practice for students, eLearning exercises).
- Machinery (automobiles, motorcycles, weapons).

But the students also choose less frequent topics such as:

- Geography (cities, geocaching).
- Games (spacecraft).
- Lifestyle (nutrition, food).
- Records of attendance at work.
- Books and libraries.

The structure of instruction and the way the tasks are assigned and evaluated lead the students to independence. This is especially evident when they work on their course credit task. Brief orientation and basic demands for their credit task are given to students in the form of written instructions. After the approval of the theme for their IS development and specification of the IS requirements, they proceed, if possible, on their own.

The important progressive phases of work (conceptual and logical model) are discussed with the teacher, and the students continue only after submitting the outcomes and obtaining the teacher's approval. The actual development tool for the implementation of IS is not presented in detail at lectures. It is up to the students to master work with MS Access; they themselves have to acquire the necessary aids. Or they may even choose other software development framework (Delphi, PHP, etc.). The submission of the course credit assignment is interactive; the students respond to the teacher's comments via electronic means of communication.

3.3 IS geocaching

The example presents an outcome of student's work in theme Geocaching', source of the example is paper. Based on the documentation of this assignment, the following parts will be presented:
- Assignment for the IS development.
- Entity Relationship diagram (ERD), Fig. 17.
- Data dictionary (DD), Tab. 17.
- Functional diagram (FD), Fig. 18.
- Relational data model (RDM), Fig. 19.
- Description of the final application.

Assignment specification: Create an information system about cashes and their owners. The cache entity is characterized by the following attributes:
- the name of the cache
- hint
- the date of creation
- the date of the last visit
- coordinates

The cache entity is further specified by the entities of type and size of the cache and the difficulty of the terrain where the cache is located. The person entity (the owner of the cache) is characterized by the following attributes:

- owners' name
- the date of creation the account
- the number of caches found

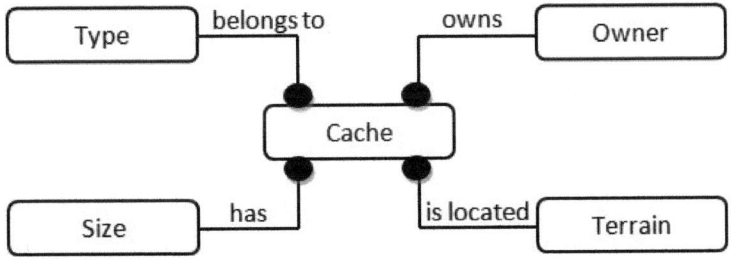

Fig. 17 Entity Relationship diagram-geocaching

Tab. 17 Data dictionary-geocaching

Entity	Attribute	Date Type	Length	Obligation	Primary Key
Cache	C_ID	Number		Y	PK
	C_Title	Text	20	Y	
	C_Hint	Text	50	N	
	C_DateCreate	Date		Y	
	C_DateVisit	Date		N	
	C_Coordinates	Text	15	Y	
Type	T_ID	Number		Y	PK
	T_Title	Text	10	Y	
Size	S_ID	Number		Y	PK
	S_Size	Text	10	Y	
Terrain	Ter_ID	Number		Y	PK
	Ter_Terrain	Number		Y	
Owner	O_ID	Number		Y	PK
	O_Name	Text	20	Y	
	O_DateCreate	Date		Y	
	O_NumFound	Number	7	N	

The IS should allow for saving, deleting, editing and searching the data from the stored data and the creation of required reports.

The IS about caches and their owners was created in MS Access DBMS. The IS provides users with convenient and clear browsing through data about cashes and their owners. To manage the database, functions for adding, deleting, and editing data are available. The program also allows the creation of reports according to selected criteria.

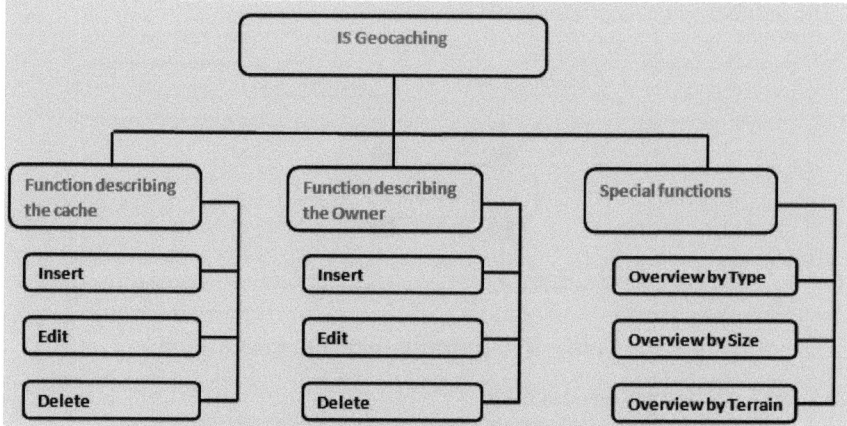

Fig. 18 Functional diagram-geocaching

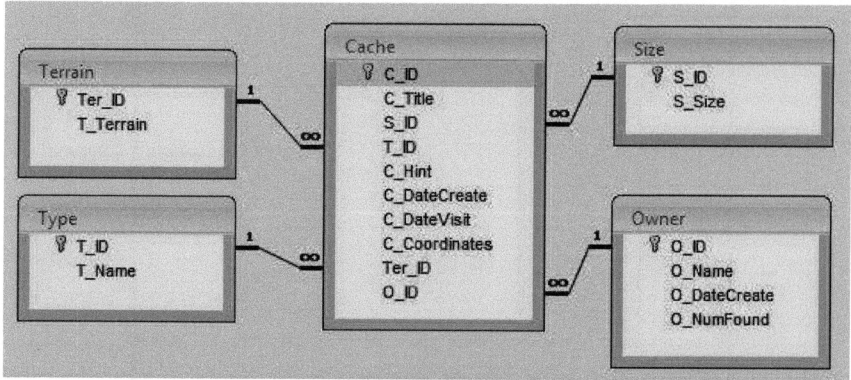

Fig. 19 Database structure on the RDM-geocaching

The main menu (see Fig. 20) offers seven function buttons. Clicking the 'Caches' button enable the users to view the data about cashes; they can be added, edited or deleted. Clicking the 'Owners' button provides the users with similar functions concerning their owners (see Fig. 21).

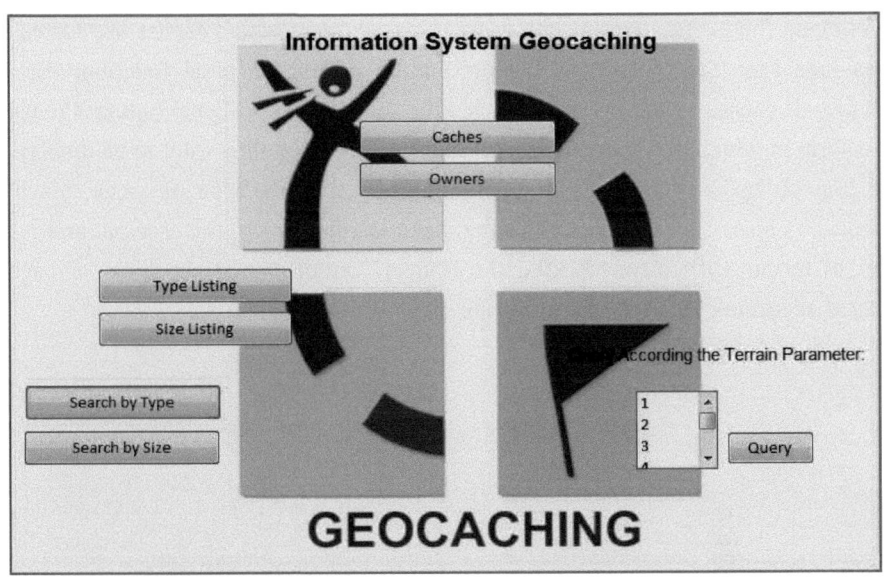

Fig. 20 User interface of the application-geocaching

C_ID ▾	C_Title ▾	S_II ▾	T_ID ▾	C_Hint ▾	C_[
3	The Hubert	2	5	In the roots	
4	Lime hill	2	3	Under a rock	
5	Helen's spring	1	1	Above	

Owner

ID: 1

Name: Bomerone

Date of Acconut Create: 10.11.2011

Number fo Caches Found: 60

Listing of Owner's Caches:

Fig. 21 Information about the owners-geocaching

By clicking the 'Type Listing', the users get a report in which caches are sorted by types (see Fig. 22). The 'Size Listing' button offers the same function; the set contains all caches sorted by size. By clicking the 'Search by Type' button, the users get a form in which they can choose the type of cache that they want to be displayed. The 'Search by Size' button has a similar function as the type of cache, but it is arranged by size. The last function of the menu is a list, where the user can select the level of terrain difficulty. Clicking the 'Query' button shows the table of caches selected according to the degree of terrain difficulty.

Type

Type	Title	Size	Terrain	Hint	Date of Creation
Traditional					
	Ash	Regular	4	Do not go to the tree	2.10.2006
	New mill	Small	2	inside the stump	18.10.2007
	Prigl	Large	4	Take a neoprene	7.12.2007
	The Hubert	Small	5	In the roots	20.8.2009
Multicache					
	Lime hill	Small	3	Under a rock	26.11.2010
	On the corner	Regular	2		20.3.2005

Fig. 22 Report on the types of cashes-geocaching

3.4 Importance and benefits

The future ICT specialists should benefit from the course by acquiring strong knowledge of basic concepts of IS, which can be further developed in their study and practice. The students do not need further expansion of the knowledge concerning the RDM in the future, which, despite all the advances in IT, is nearly 100% presented in current DBMS.

The importance of the course for 'business' oriented students lies in obtaining comprehensive theoretical information and practical experience in IS and its development. Certainly, the subject contributes to the students' ability to document the results of their work and to work independently on an assignment. An important benefit of the course is the development of students' ability to work independently and to document the results of their work.

49

In both groups of students, the evaluation of the documentation of their IS is aimed at encouraging students to work professionally with a text editor. It is truly surprising that most of our secondary schools graduates are not ready to create quality documents and are very poorly trained in the use of the office automation software.

The example summarizes the experience in teaching the foundations of IS. By stepwise refinement of the content and process of teaching, the course has reached the stage which guarantees its stability with the useful pieces of knowledge gained from methodological procedures applied, including the activation of students and their independent work development.

An illustrative example of student's work is presented without any corrections. The students' feedback on the course is positive; they appreciate the opportunity to become familiar with one of the approaches to IS development, and are grateful for the strong knowledge concerning the theory of IS modelling. The preparation of undergraduate students includes the described course as an introduction to the study. So far, the students have received education in general subjects only and their expectations are set high. We can state that their ideas were met. They have obtained substantial foundations for further education in IS and gained deep interest in the study program.

4 Research regarding the IS education

The pedagogical research regarding the IS education was completed in the 'Information Management' course, oriented to the education of the IS development for the business oriented students at the Magister's level Faculty of management and economics, University of Tomas Bata (UTB) in Zlín, Czech Republic. At the end of the course, a detailed survey of the students' opinions on the content, importance and quality of the course was carried out.

The crucial issue in focus in information management are IS. However, filling in boxes in a business case in a commercial IS does not facilitate the deep understanding of the IS. The importance, options and operation of an IS are best understood when you create your own IS.

4.1 Structure and content of the course

KIMA – 'Information Management' is an optional course for students of the distance study programme. KIMA was selected in year 2012 by 31 students. Out of these, 15 (48%) studied Management and Marketing, and 16 (52%) Industrial Engineering. The course was planned for 15 hours, which were regularly divided into 3 consultations.

At the first consultation, the students were asked about the reason for selecting the course. Out of 24 students attending, 22 responded to the question; see Tab. 18.

Tab. 18 Reasons for selecting the course

Ord.	Reason for selecting	Num.	%
1	Interest in IT/IS/enterprise IS	11	50
2	The only interesting elective course	4	18
3	To avoid econometrics	3	14
4	Continuity of subjects	1	5
5	Electronic enterprise	1	5
6	Relation to management	1	5
7	Merit for the field of study	1	5
	TOTAL	**22**	**100**

Based on preliminary considerations on the focus of the course, the areas of study were specified and divided into lessons with respect to the number of hours allocated to the course. The lessons included the topic of information management, geared to the creation of IS and other topics related to the IS issues.

Lessons:
1. Introduction to the topic.
2. Concepts of IS and methodology of their creation.
3. IS modelling and credit work, assignment and specifications.
4. IS analysis (ERD, FS, DS models).
5. IS design (RDM models) and the transformation of the ERD to RDM.
6. IS creation (description of MS Access and its objects).
7. Application of enterprise informatics.
8. Implementation projects/changes of IS.
9. Business intelligence, data warehouse.
10. Data mining.
11. Outsourcing, cloud computing.

During the first consultation, lessons 1 to 7 were presented. The content of the second consultation was an exercise aimed at developing one's own IS. In the third consultation, lessons 8-11 were presented and the credit session was conducted. For the successful fulfilment of the credit assignment the students were provided with the following information:

- Course credit requirements.
- Lectures and the process of the IS creation.
- Instructions for working with MS Access.
- A sample of the credit assignment and an IS final application.

4.2 Course requirements and results achieved

The course concludes with a graded credit, which can be obtained after the students hand in their credit assignment. The credit assignment can be submitted in two versions:
1. The IS analysis and design without its application in MS Access; grade E.
2. One's own IS in MS Access with the description of its creation and result; grade C.

Tab. 19 Processes of the IS development

1. Proposal of the IS theme and its specifications.	Word; IS description
2. Approval of the IS theme by the tutor.	E-mail
3. Survey for verifying the user's requirements.	Word; IS description
4. Entity-relationship diagram (ERD).	Word; IS description
5. Data dictionary (DD).	Excel; IS description
6. Functional scheme (FS).	Word; IS description
7. Transformation of the ERD to RDM.	Word; IS description
8. Modification of DD to RDM.	Word; IS description
9. Completion of the IS description (for E grade).	IS description
10. Submitting the result to the teacher (for E grade).	IS description; E-mail
11. Creation of the data base (DB).	Access; IS
12. Definition of the DB structure.	Access; IS
13. Creation of relations in the DB scheme.	Access; IS; IS description
14. Entering data in the data sheet.	Access; IS
15. Creating forms for the tables.	Access; IS
16. Inserting data from the forms.	Access; IS
17. The main form.	Access; IS
18. Creating queries and forms according to FS.	Access; IS
19. Creating reports by FS.	Access; IS
20. Linking forms, queries and reports with the menu.	Access; IS; IS description
21. Completing the IS description (for C grade).	IS; IS description
22. Submitting the result to the tutor (for C grade).	IS; IS description; E-mail

Tab. 20 Study results based on statistics

Ord.	Issue in focus	Number	%	Note
1	Total of students enrolled	31		
2	Consultation attendance (3)	24, 15, 12		
3	Surveys submitted	22/*	82	/* only out of the number of
4	Not given credit	4	13	students, who were given
5	Given credit	27	87	credit
6	- grades A/B/C/D/E	2/2/10/7/6	7/7/38/26/22	

Grades can be improved based on the result of examination (voluntarily). The creation process was specified in detail; see Tab. 19. The Tab. 20 shows the study results.

4.3 Instruction and research methodology

The course begins with the analysis of the IS issues. The following topics are covered: the concept of IS, its meaning and classification, data - information – knowledge and the database system. Then follows the teaching of the IS modelling.

Tab. 21 Survey on the KIMA course

Survey on the KIMA course

1. Did the KIMA course meet your expectations?		
☐ totally	☐ partly	☐ least
2. WHY did KIMA (not) meet your expectations?		
3. The main content of KIMA – the creation of one's own IS is for the course:		
☐ appropriate	☐ I don't know	☐ not appropriate
4. WHY is the creation of one's own IS (not) appropriate for the course?		
5. Do you recommend maintaining this content in KIMA?		
☐ yes	☐ I don't know	☐ no
6. Evaluation of the 'IS analysis – conceptual modelling' part of the course:		
☐ easy	☐ moderately difficult	☐ difficult
7. Evaluation of the 'IS design – logical modelling':		
☐ easy	☐ moderately difficult	☐ difficult
8. Evaluation of the 'IS creation – working with MS Access':		
☐ easy	☐ moderately difficult	☐ difficult
9. Did you study something similar in the previous courses at UTB?		
☐ yes	☐ approximately	☐ no
10. What are you taking away from the course for the completion of your study at UTB?		
11. What are you taking away from the course for practice?		
12. Evaluate your tutor:		
☐ excellent	☐ average	☐ poor
13. Recommendation for your tutor.		
14. Any other comment about the course?		

It includes the topics of the IS model, general principles of modelling, IS life cycle, explanation of methodology - method - technique - tool.

Then a structured approach to the IS development and a conceptual level of modelling are introduced. This part can be described as the core for understanding the field and the proper basis for analytical thinking of an IS creator. The structured methodology (levels and dimensions of modelling, application of general approaches to modelling, a conceptual level model) are explained. The constructs and rules of the ERD, FS and DD are presented.

After that an explanation of the MS Access functions follows, as well as an example of its use; then starts the creation and description of the IS. Along with rethinking the teaching methodology, the way of researching the relationship of students to the subject and its future development was also considered. The research methodology consisted of observation, discussion, and, in particular, of the development and implementation of the final survey. The survey (see

Grades can be improved based on the result of examination (voluntarily). The creation process was specified in detail; see Tab. 19. The Tab. 20 shows the study results.

4.4 Instruction and research methodology

The course begins with the analysis of the IS issues. The following topics are covered: the concept of IS, its meaning and classification, data - information – knowledge and the database system. Then follows the teaching of the IS modelling.

Tab. 21) contains questions pertaining to the relationship of the student to the course and its importance for their study and practice. Most of the items are closed questions; the open questions seek the reasons for the student's evaluation and describe his/her views.

4.5 Results of the survey in KIMA

Here follows the evaluation based on the survey. The survey was anonymous in the paper-and-pencil form. Some students were responding when taking their credit test. However, many students sent their credit assignments as well as their responses by e-mail, but these were not examined by the teacher immediately; they were printed and filed with the other ones.

1. Did the KIMA course meet your expectations?
totally: 16 (74%)   partly: 5 (22%) least: 1 (4%)

2a. WHY did KIMA meet your expectations?
Everything that was described in the curriculum was fulfilled.
I learnt something new.
Creation of one's own IS – 4x.
Working with MS Access – 2x.

2b. WHY did KIMA not meet your expectations?
To explain the procedure of the IS creation in a more detailed way.

The course required more independent work than I expected.
To devote more time to MS Access.
To use more sophisticated program than MS Access.
Not everybody owns MS Access – 2x.

3. The content of KIMA – the creation of one's own IS is for the course:
appropriate: 21 (96 %)   I don't know: 1 (4%)   not appropriate: 0

4. WHY is the creation of one's own IS appropriate for the course?
Practical work with databases, creating IS – 4x.
Course content reflects reality.
Deepening the knowledge of theory.
Developing analytical thinking.
Solving one's own example.

5. Do you recommend maintaining this content in KIMA?
yes: 16 (74%)   I don't know: 3 (13%)   no: 3 (13%)

6. Evaluation of the 'IS analysis – conceptual modelling':
easy: 6 (28%)   moderately difficult: 13 (59%)   difficult: 3 (13%)

7. Evaluation of the 'IS design – logical modelling':
easy: 5 (22%)   moderately difficult: 14 (65%)   difficult: 3 (13%)

8. Evaluation of the 'IS creation – working with MS Access':
easy: 10 (46%) moderately difficult: 11 (50%)   difficult: 1 (4%)

9. Did you have something similar in the previous courses at UTB?
yes: 6 (28%)   I don't know: 9 (41%)   no: 7 (31%)

10. What are you taking away from the course for the completion of your study at UTB?
Working with MS Access – 9x.
Overview on the IS creation – 7x.
Improvement in MS Excel.
Course credit.
Revision for the final state exam.
Understanding data mining.
New information.

11. What are you taking away from the course for practice?
Working with MS Access – 7x.
Overview on the IS creation, specifications – 10x.

12. Evaluate your tutor:
excellent: 20 (92%) average: 2 (8%) poor: 0

13. Recommendation for your tutor:
There is nothing to be changed in the course.
Keep going. Strong nerves.
I'd like to meet such teachers in other courses.
Beyond reproach, fast communication.
Satisfaction with the content of the course.
No objections.

More focus on practical work within the course.
Less independent work should be required.

14. Another comment on the course?
Satisfaction. Thank you.
Excellent organization, the willingness of the teacher.
A very useful course.
To add an introduction of a system
Even the looser form was suitable; yet I took away important pieces of knowledge.
It meets expectations; but I won't most likely use it in practice.

4.6 Summarization

The chapter summarizes the author's experience in the teaching the foundations of IS development in the KIMA course for business oriented students. The instruction is based on the long experience of teaching IS to computer science students, but it is modified to the needs of business oriented students. Teaching methodology includes the modelling procedure of an IS, its design and creation in MS Access. The creation of the IS is well along with other lectures on information management in the enterprise environment.

Based on the evaluation of the course, with an emphasis on the views of students, it is suitable to maintain and develop the Information Management course for business oriented students, to edit its content, structure and organization according to the comments received in the survey.

A number of universities teach IS with different goals, such as a mere introduction, modelling and development, implementation and operation, integration, security, etc., at both general and professional levels. Teaching IS is designed not only for computer science experts, but also for business students. IS is a topic where you can conveniently share different approaches and experiences and to use available information to carry out joint research projects.

Also, a targeted research on teaching IS would be beneficial; it would verify the applied methodologies, techniques and tools, forms of the teaching process, communication methods, the use of learning resources and other elements of teaching. The research on teaching is mostly conducted at faculties of education, and it is focused on general issues of educational theory and practice.

Conclusions

The aim of the manuscript is to summarize the experience gained from teaching the basics of IS. There is presented the theoretical basis of teaching and the methodological process in order to achieve maximum benefit for students.

The publication can be used for study and for educational purposes, and its author will be grateful for any feedback. Have a pleasant study!

Prof. Ladislav BURITA, ladislav.burita@unob.cz

University of Defence, 66210 Brno, Kounicova 65, Czech Republic and

University of Tomas Bata in Zlín, 76001 Zlín, Mostní 5139, Czech Republic

References

[1] Bruce, T. A. *Designing Quality Databases with IDEF1X Information Models.* New York, US: Dorset House Publishing, 1992.

[2] BURITA, Ladislav. Approach to teaching information systems – one year after. In: *Information and Communication Technology in Education.* Ostrava, Czech Republic: University of Ostrava, Pedagogical Faculty, 2013, p. 66-75.

[3] BURITA, Ladislav. Teaching Methodology of Information Systems. In: *Proceedings of the 4th International Conference on Computer Supported Education, Vol. 2.* Porto, Portugal: Institute for Systems and Technologies of Information, Control and Communication, 2012, p. 179-182.

[4] BURITA, Ladislav, ONDRYHAL, Vojtěch, TRUNDA, Michal, HODICKÝ, Jan. *Informační podpora v resortu obrany (Information support in military branches).* Prague, Czech Republic: Ministry of Defence – Agency of the military information and services, 2006.

[5] *CA Erwin Data Modeller Community Edition.* Available at https://www.ca.com/us/register/forms/ca-erwin-data-modeler-community - edition-evaluation-software.aspx

[6] Codd, E. F. A relations mode of data for large shared data banks. *CACM,* 1970, vol 13, 6, p. 377-387.

[7] Giannocarro, R. at al. *A Structured Methodology for Developing Performance Measures in any Environment.* Available at http://maja.uni-mb.si/files/apem/APEM2-2_91-99.pdf

[8] *Integration Definition for Information Modelling (IDEF1X).* Federal Information Processing Standards Publication 184, the US National Institute of Standards and Technology. December 21, 1993. Available at http://www.idef.com/pdf/idef1x.pdf

[9] Pokorný, J. *Databázové systémy a jejich použití v informačních systémech. (Database systems and its using in the information systems).* Prague, Czech Republic: Academia, 1992.

[10] Scheber, A. *Dátabázové systémy. (Database systems).* Bratislava, Slovak: ALFA, 1988.

[11] Tsichritzis, D.C., Lochovsky, F.H. *Databázové systémy. (Database systems).* Prague, Czech Republic: SNTL, 1987.

Printed by Books on Demand GmbH, Norderstedt / Germany